# BigTime® Piano

## Jazz & Blues

2011 Edition

**Level 4**
**Intermediate**

Arranged by

**Nancy and Randall Faber**

Production Coordinator: Jon Ophoff
Design and Illustration: Terpstra Design, San Francisco
Engraving: Dovetree Productions, Inc.

**FABER**
PIANO ADVENTURES®
3042 Creek Drive
Ann Arbor, Michigan 48108

# A NOTE TO TEACHERS

**BigTime® Piano Jazz & Blues** is a great collection of jazz and blues pieces. Standards such as *Take the "A" Train* and *Desafinado* provide an introduction to basic jazz styles such as swing and bossa nova. Other moods and styles are featured in classics such as *Autumn Leaves, Misty,* and *Night Train,* and in original compositions such as *Equinox* and *Big City Blues.* The book is arranged for the intermediate-level pianist and is especially written to create a "big" sound while remaining within the level.

**BigTime® Piano Jazz & Blues** is part of the *BigTime® Piano* series arranged by Faber and Faber. As the name implies, this level marks a point of significant achievement for the piano student.

Following are the levels of the supplementary library, which lead from *PreTime®* to *BigTime®*.

| | |
|---|---|
| PreTime® Piano | (Primer Level) |
| PlayTime® Piano | (Level 1) |
| ShowTime® Piano | (Level 2A) |
| ChordTime® Piano | (Level 2B) |
| FunTime® Piano | (Level 3A – 3B) |
| BigTime® Piano | (Level 4) |

Each level offers books in a variety of styles, making it possible for the teacher to offer stimulating material for every student. For a complimentary detailed listing, e-mail faber@pianoadventures.com or write us at the mailing address below.

Visit **www.PianoAdventures.com**.

**Helpful Hints:**

1. Many jazz and blues pieces use swing rhythm. Here the quarter note is divided into a long eighth note followed by a short eighth note, rather than being equally divided. It is approximately the same as ♩♪. Where swing is indicated in the tempo mark, the ♫'s or ♫'s should be played as swung eighth notes rather than interpreted literally.

2. Many blues tunes use variations of a common chord progression known as the 12-bar blues. Students with an elementary harmony background can be taught the chord pattern easily and should learn to recognize it. The pattern is as follows:

| I | I | I | I |
|---|---|---|---|
| IV | IV | I | I |
| V | IV | I | I |

3. Attention should be given to dynamics, pedaling and tone to create an artistic performance, just as in "serious" music.

**About Jazz & Blues**

Jazz and blues are distinctively American styles of music, characterized by improvisation and syncopated rhythm. Blues—an ancestor of jazz—can be traced back to the days of slavery, when American blacks began to combine African melodies and rhythms with Western harmony.

At the turn of the century, ragtime's syncopated rhythm took the country by storm—in fact Scott Joplin's piano rags were best sellers in his day. As blues and ragtime styles influenced each other, a dynamic swing style emerged which eventually became known as jazz. Championed in New Orleans by Jelly Roll Morton and Louis Armstrong, the new sound soared in popularity. By the 1920s, jazz had entered the mainstream of American popular music.

During the Swing Era of the 1930s and 40s, people were dancing to the big band sounds of Glenn Miller and other band leaders. The cool sounds of bebop followed in the 1950s, a time when solo artists such as Miles Davis and Charlie Parker infused jazz with a new seriousness—and ever since then jazz has continued to grow and change. Today the influence of blues and jazz can be heard in almost all popular music.

ISBN 978-1-61677-011-2

# TABLE OF CONTENTS

# Take the "A" Train

Words and Music by
**BILLY STRAYHORN**

# Autumn Leaves

**English lyrics by JOHNNY MERCER**
**French lyrics by JACQUES PREVERT**

Music by
**JOSEPH KOSMA**

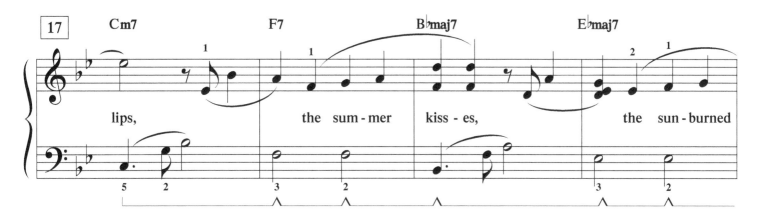

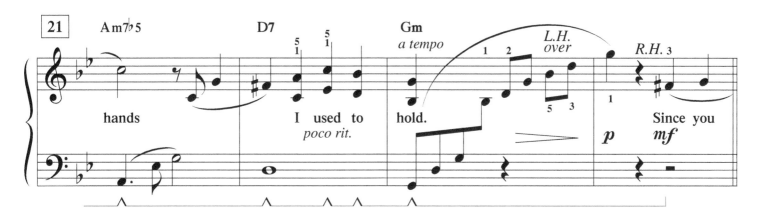

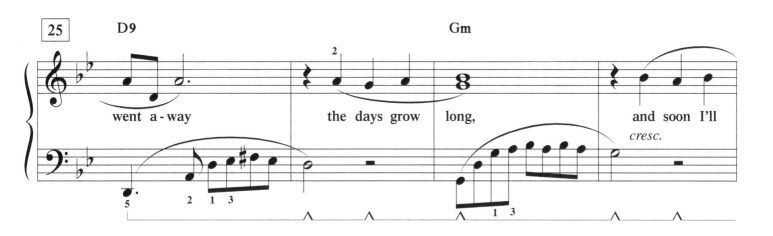

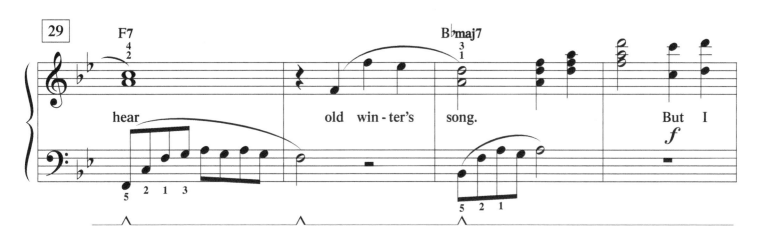

# Georgia on My Mind

Lyrics by
STUART GORRELL

Music by
HOAGY CARMICHAEL

# Satin Doll

Words by
**JOHNNY MERCER**
**and BILLY STRAYHORN**

Music by
**DUKE ELLINGTON**

15

FF1011

# Big City Blues

NANCY FABER

# Cast Your Fate to the Wind

Lyrics by CAREL WERBER
Music by VINCE GUARALDI

# Misty

Words by
**JOHNNY BURKE**

Music by
**ERROLL GARNER**

# Locomotive Blues

**Moving steadily, no swing**

RANDALL FABER

# Lullaby of Birdland

Words by GEORGE DAVID WEISS
Music by GEORGE SHEARING

# Perdido

ERVIN DRAKE, HARRY LENK,
and JUAN TIZOL

# Desafinado

Original lyrics by NEWTON MENDONCA
Music by ANTONIO CARLOS JOBIM

# Night Train

JIMMY FORREST,
OSCAR WASHINGTON,
and LEWIS C. SIMPKINS

FF1011

32

FF1011

# Equinox

NANCY FABER

# All the Things You Are

Lyrics by
**OSCAR HAMMERSTEIN II**

Music by
**JEROME KERN**

# A Taste of Honey

Words by
RIC MARLOW

Music by
BOBBY SCOTT